You're All Washed Up, Beetle Bailey

Here's another in the happy series of books based on one of the most famous comic strips in the country. Once again the madcap inmates of Camp Swampy valiantly strive to overcome their own ineptitude—and succeed in delighting us on every page.

Mort Walker again gives us a barrel of laughs in his marvelous cartoons concerning the most unprofessional soldier in the army!

Beetle Bailey Books

YOU'RE ALL WASHED UP,

Mort Walker

CHARTER BOOKS, NEW YORK

YOU'RE ALL WASHED UP, BEETLE BAILEY

A Charter Book published by arrangement with
King Features Syndicate, Inc.

PRINTING HISTORY
Charter Original / March 1985

ISBN: 0-441-05298-3

Charter Books are published by The Berkley Publishing Group
200 Madison Avenue, New York, New York 10016.
PRINTED IN THE UNITED STATES OF AMERICA

11-16

12-15